hi hi hi hi indiany

AF176111

Peter Oberfrank – Hunziker

Impressum:

Bibliografische Information der Deutschen Nationalbibliothek: Die Deutsche Nationalbibliothek verzeichnet diese Publikation in der Deutschen Nationalbibliografie; detaillierte bibliografische Daten sind im Internet über www.dnb.de abrufbar.

© 2022 Peter Oberfrank – Hunziker
Herstellung und Verlag
BoD – Books on Demand, Norderstedt

ISBN 9783756224456

My written unique creative funny book by me
Peter Oberfrank – Hunziker with the joyfull
indiany creative artyfull booktiteling
„hi hi hi hi indiany
Peter Oberfrank – Hunziker" is celebrating
ever grande cheerio and I Peter Oberfrank -
Hunziker am NHL icehockeyplayer ever and
technical working ever and manly ever and
worldwide indiany and unique indiany and I
Peter Oberfrank - Hunziker am ever with my
weddingly Michelle Hunziker and our five
funny children indianyly Miri Hunziker and
indianyly Liri Hunziker and indianyly Tiri
Hunziker and indianyly Amelie Hunziker and
indianyly Linea Hunziker and we are
worldwide journeying and unique christmas
celebrating and presenting ever and I Peter
Oberfrank - Hunziker am with all my NHL art
naming liking NHL 24 Christian Perthaler and
NHL 20 Henrique Lundquvist and NHL 19
Steve Yzerman and NHL 8 Ovechkin and
NHL 16 Kevin Lavallee and NHL

Modano and

NHL Malkin

and NHL Krutov

and NHL 71 Brad Isbister

and NHL 47 Martin St. Louis
tampy

and NHL happy joyy and NHL Joe Thornton
and NHL 9 Adrian Kempe and nhling
icehockey indiany and NHL great perthalerlen
at Alpensee indiany and NHL Filip Chytil and
NHL 99 Wayne Gretzky and all my 32 NHL
teams

New York Rangers
newyorky
NHL icehockey stary indiany
as most valuable NHL (National Hockey
League, Nature History League, National
History League) icehockey franchise ever and
great blueshirts celebrating indiany
NHL icehockey grande Stanley museum
indiany
Peter Oberfrank – Hunziker

New York Islanders
Islanders are highlanders
spacy center indiany
Peter Oberfrank – Hunziker

New Jersey Devils

Devils icehockey is great NHL icehockey and american partying indiany
fashion clothing shows indiany
reataurants with nice eating and drinking
dancing palaces indiany
NHL museum
NHL shop
NHL stadium series indiany
sportying
artistic
NHL series
NHL ranking ever
holidaying
creative art
indiany
holidaying
ceremonying
icehockey playing
NHL is a League and I Peter Oberfrank – Hunziker am captainying all my 32 NHL teams with my art naming indiany
NHL circus indiany
Peter Oberfrank – Hunziker

Edmonton Oilers
NHL classico icehockey indiany
Oilers are Hoilers
great NHL marketing indiany
sportying indiany
Peter Oberfrank – Hunziker

Tampa Bay Lightning
tampy *** indiany
Great celebrations with NHL National Hockey
League icehockeysport and celebrating with
my indiany NHL icehockeyteam ever NHL
icehockey Stanley cup titels in years 2004 and
2020 and 2021 and ever being with my NHL
art naming NHL 79 Ross Colton and great
partying indiany Peter Oberfrank – Hunziker

Colorado Avalanche
great NHL icehockey with ever my also
captainying NHL art naming NHL 29 Nathan
MacKinnon and superior icehockeyplaying
and high levelling and ceremonies indiany and
great winning of NHL National Hockey
League icehockey Presidents trophy in year
2021 with my american indiany NHL team
Colorado Avalanche indiany
 Peter Oberfrank – Hunziker

Florida Panthers
NHL icehockey with great icehockeysport
indiany and creative celebrating the winning
with my indiany art NHL icehockeyteam
Florida Panthers and being NHL Presidents
trophy winning team in year 2022 and easy
beachying partying pantherlen indiany with
my NHL art naming liking NHL Joe Thornton
and NHL 28 Claude Giroux and my original
naming
Peter Oberfrank – Hunziker

great celebrations

disco party

music party

sportying party

happy party indiany
Peter Oberfrank – Hunziker

indiany party
Peter Oberfrank – Hunziker

Calgary Flames
NHL happy party
great NHL National Hockey League museum
for great scoring quality indiany and sportying
and celebrating
indiany
Peter Oberfrank – Hunziker

Nashville Predators
grande beach indiany
NHL icehockey sportying
indiany
Peter Oberfrank – Hunziker

Chicago Blackhawks
creative indiany
NHL tropheum indiany
nhling icehockey indiany
NHL fanfaren music indiany
Peter Oberfrank – Hunziker

Detroit Red wings
Detroity indiany
NHL wingerlen icehockey and celebrating
with happy partying and sportying indiany
Peter Oberfrank – Hunziker

Dallas Stars
NHL icehockey show stars indiany
Peter Oberfrank – Hunziker

Los Angeles Kings
NHL icehockey kingsy and beach parties
indiany
Peter Oberfrank – Hunziker

Vancouver Canucks
NHL icehockey puck museum indiany
Peter Oberfrank – Hunziker

Minnesota Wild Stars
with great landscape and NHL icehockey
playing creative and farm team Iowa Wild
indiany
Peter Oberfrank – Hunziker

Montreal Canadiens
NHL icehockey record champions indiany
NHL pin museum
Kindergarten
Yoga
NHL Hall of fame indiany
great art
indiany
Peter Oberfrank – Hunziker

Arizona Coyotes
NHL sports stadium with great icehockeysport
and dschungel county indiany
Peter Oberfrank – Hunziker

Boston Bruins
NHL great icehockey and museum parties
indiany
Peter Oberfrank – Hunziker

Ottawa Senators
NHL superior icehockey and NHL great
icehockey and NHL creative icehockey and
festival indiany Peter Oberfrank – Hunziker

Anaheim Ducks
easy great NHL icehockey and creative party
and NHL conferencing indiany
Peter Oberfrank – Hunziker

Buffalo Sabres
NHL worldwide icehockey touring and celebrating indiany
Peter Oberfrank – Hunziker

San Jose Sharks
NHL icehockey sharky museum indiany and
sportying parties indiany
Peter Oberfrank – Hunziker

Winnipeg Jets
NHL icehockey with style indiany
Peter Oberfrank – Hunziker

Toronto Maple Leafs
NHL icehockey toronto stary indiany
Peter Oberfrank – Hunziker

Carolina Hurricanes
NHL icehockey with grande ceremonying
indiany
Peter Oberfrank – Hunziker

Columbus Blue Jackets
NHL icehockey and happy partying 13 hours
and celebrations ever with happy partying
indiany Peter Oberfrank – Hunziker

Philadelphia Flyers
worldwide NHL icehockeysport indiany and
colourfull NHL jersey parties indiany
Peter Oberfrank – Hunziker

Pittsburgh Penguins
NHL stary icehockey worldwide and creative
icehockeyplaying indiany and celebrations
indiany
Peter Oberfrank – Hunziker

Washington Capitals
I Peter Oberfrank – Hunziker like being with
my NHL art naming NHL 8 Ovechkin and
NHL Washingtoni indiany and great winning
of NHL icehockey Stanley cup title in year
2018 with my indiany icehockey team NHL
Washington Capitals and ever partying indiany
Washingtoni indiany
Peter Oberfrank – Hunziker

NHL shield indiany museum indiany
Peter Oberfrank – Hunziker

creative
Peter Oberfrank – Hunziker

St. Louis Blues
NHL icehockey with great art indiany
I Peter Oberfrank – Hunziker like being with
my NHL art names liking NHL Pietrangelo
and Backes and NHL joky indiany

beach and music party
indiany
Peter Oberfrank – Hunziker

Las Vegas Golden Knights
NHL unique icehockeysport indiany
worldwide indiany
Peter Oberfrank – Hunziker

Seattle Kraken
NHL icehockey with systemic indiany
icehockeyplaying and indiany celebrating
indiany
Peter Oberfrank – Hunziker

NHL all sports indiany center

colourfull buildy

beach ressort

NHL celebrations indiany
Peter Oberfrank – Hunziker

NHL stary icehockey with great sport indiany
Peter Oberfrank – Hunziker

NHL icehockey sportying indiany
Peter Oberfrank – Hunziker

NHL (National Hockey League, Nature
History League, National History League)
Washingtoni indiany
Peter Oberfrank – Hunziker

celebrations

Peter Oberfrank – Hunziker

nice

NHL WU 59 icehockey champions indiany

WOW

NHL icehockey stadium series indiany
Peter Oberfrank – Hunziker

NHL memorandum indiany
Peter Oberfrank – Hunziker

NHL icehockeyshield indiany
Peter Oberfrank – Hunziker

and newyorky and CSKA Moscow and
Makarov and Larionov and HSV Hamburger
Sportverein and Ernst Happel and NHL
Madison Square Garden New York indiany
and NHL Rockefeller center indiany and

NHL cheerio pin indiany and Stankiewic and
Dennis Houle and Bykov and Taylor Hall and
Vigneault and Jeff Gorton and Pavelski and
NHL Washington academy and skyblue and
worldwide journeying indiany and NHL
Heatley and NHL 87 Sydney Crosby and team
Canada and olympic champions indiany and
historical and NHL Carolina Hurricanes
indiany and NHL 21 Niederreiter and Kerth
and Klinsmann and Tichonov and Tretjak and
Fedorov and Fetisov and forever and NHL
indiany and NHL indiany sign and NHL shield
and indiany and hearty indiany

and NHL tampylen indiany

and Vasilvesky and Goudet and Stamkos and
NHL 4 Neil Belland and NHL Panarin and
NHL 14 Greg Holst and NHL icehockey
museum indiany and NHL Dury and VfB
Stuttgart and Hansi Müller and OEHV indiany
and ÖFB indiany and NHL jury and NHL
board indiany and NHL Nödl and ECR and
Graz 99 ers and NHL trading indiany NHL 28
Claude Giroux and NHL contracting indiany
and NHL playery cards indiany and NHL Pertl
indiany and great running and NHL Las Vegas
Golden Knights stars indiany and glanzvoll
and sporty running and NHL 23 Marco Rossi
and austrian and NHL icehockey confetti party
indiany and

I Peter Oberfrank – Hunziker am american
indiany and worldwide captainying all my
NHL teams ever and winning more than
100.000.000.000.000 NHL icehockeygames
and great ever partying indiany
Peter Oberfrank – Hunziker

 and NHL all stars trophy indiany and FC
Bayern München and cooly indiany and
greeny and NHL stary indiany

and sportying

and joy indiany and cultural and ZSC Lions
and SC Rapperswil-Jona and EKZ Zeller
Eisbären Zell am See and KAC and Gösser EV
and team Argentina and Diego Armando
Maradona and FIFA world champion indiany
and museum natural NFL Tom Brady and
manly ever and NHL Kopitar and NHL star
indiany and Real Madrid and CF Barcelona
and Estadio Atzteka and nation teams and
NBA basketball and NFL american football
and MLB baseball and skiing and tennis
playing and sportsgymnastic and NHL
celebrations indiany and NHL 18 Patrick Kane
and NHL happy creative indiany and NHLY
museums indiany and buildy and Pueblo and
Calgary buildy and Edmonti buildy indiany
and grande cheerio indiany
Peter Oberfrank – Hunziker

and NHL Phili indiany and NHL jerseys
indiany and hiking and technical working
indiany and NHL music parties indiany and
worldwide languaging indiany and book and
all books and NHL Weihnachtsbuch and NHL
winterwonderlandy indiany and NHL working
indiany and NHL kingsy indiany and NHL
creative indiany and joky and easy and Love
pantherlen beachying indiany and stary NHL

indiany and celebrating and

NHL network indiany and remembering and
all sports and I Peter Oberfrank – Hunziker am
NHL National Hockey League icehockey
Stanley cup champions ever with all my NHL
teams ever and great winning NHL icehockey
Presidents trophy ever

and NHLY indiany and Rapidlauf indiany and
NHL Washingtoni indiany and
NHL Kelchy indiany
and NHL indiany sign and

creative

and New York

and Chicago

and Berlin

and Hamburg

and Mexiko

and Graz

and Chiemsee

and Los Angeles

and Washington

and Calgary

and Florida

and Moscow

and Columbus city

and New York Island indiany

and Vancouver

and Pittsburgh state city indiany

and Stockholm

and Klagenfurt

and Wien

and Zürich

and München
Red Bull parties indiany
Peter Oberfrank – Hunziker

and Dresden
NHL book indiany
Peter Oberfrank – Hunziker

and New Jersey indiany

and Zell am See

and Tampa Bay
tampy NHL *** tampy icehockey stars
indiany
Peter Oberfrank – Hunziker

and Dallas

and Columbia state indiany

and nature land

and Philadelphia city indiany
Peter Oberfrank – Hunziker

and Chicago indiany
Peter Oberfrank – Hunziker

and great ceremonying with my NHL indiany
icehockeyteam Tampa Bay Lightning indiany
Peter Oberfrank – Hunziker

NHL icehockey Champions trophy indiany

creative indiany and grande cheerio and
champe and unique worldwide happy indiany
Peter Oberfrank - Hunziker